Chat Rooms is an all inclusive literary focused open mic and independent publisher located in Everett, WA. Find us at Lucky Dime every Wednesday.

Est. 2023

BOOK OF
OF
AINT

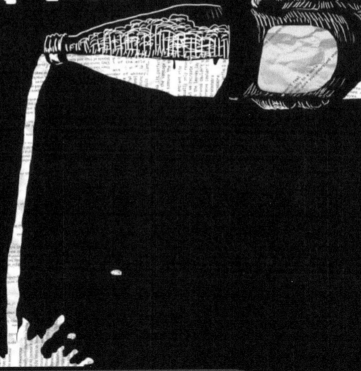

Published by Chat Rooms in Everett, WA

ISBN: 978-1-0881-7722-8

Cover Art by Dylan Speeg

Cobain Triptych Art by J.T. Dockery

Interior Design by Tex Gresham

Edited by Graham Isaac, Mark Flanigan, and Will Toedtman.

The Book of Ain't

Michael Crossley

This collection is dedicated to the memory of

Charles Whittington

Foreword

The sound of the poet roams through the landscape from Ohio to Montana to New Orleans to San Franciso to old Mexico to various Parts Unknown (and even some Parts Known) & back again, landing (mostly) in North of West ("where conifers utterly overwhelm their broader leafed brethren / dog lichen and cascara / salal and basalt / sitka shooting roots down into the shallow / soil, loose under the rocks"). Like a marriage of Rimbaud & Frances Farmer, or: a marriage of Whitman & "the Satanik girls of Instagram" (if not a Marriage of Heaven & Hell), Crossley's Book ov Ain't presents the / a / one epic poem of the final Americas that narrates the deconstruction of transcending all the destruction, the (despite all the) complication-contradiction-amputation-collection-of-occasions (Americans--and maybe just humans, as a group of hairless apes--only survive to narrate by writing from and in that space/place & usually writing through to outside if not beyond time).

I just happened to look out my window while writing this and in a quick-flash observed two doves doing the

1

act (it was a quick-flash, indeed) that (possibly/eventually) makes for the replication of more doves on an early spring afternoon, which reminds me that Crossley's poetics are concerned with a continuum, however disrupted, broken, or even delirious (something poets from Theodore Roethke to Frank Stanford to Prince would recognize, I must suspect, although what I suspect is my suspicion is simply: fact). What Crossley's book of not poems but of poem within his / the one poem of Ain't does primarily (but not only) is remind me of a question it never hit me to ask until I read Crossley's words & received the answer, so that I may only now ask the question now, already knowing: what if Charles Olson & Johnny Thunders together wrote a libretto for an opera concerned with investigating occult Seattle on mission to solve the riddle of the Sphinx by solving the riddle of the looming symbol of (the Self-Annihilated) Kurt Cobain?

Ah of Aleph. Alpha. Ah-Numa. Suspir-Ah. Poetri-Ah. Divinit-Ah. Sacr-Ah. Nil as in: Babylonia/Mayan. Sanskrit as in Sunya. Vi as in: to swell. Sifr/Arabic: the root of zero & cypher. Decartes: proof of God in the meeting point of: invinite vs. void = zero. The balance point of negative vs. positive. This is all leading to me to applying (some of) my studies regarding what that could be of Self-Annihillation, which is to say also: of Ain't.

Full disclosure: I've been in conversation with Crossley's poetics since the 90s when we both were barely more than 19 in some place the Shawnee never called "Kentucky," until I thought that the poet became a dead man in the early 21st century (to be fair, I've died a few times, myself) only to discover that same man a few more years later in another decade walking Seattle like Lazarus--putting the tongue back in washing--with a folio of fresh verse under his arm as if he'd not only never died but actually ascended while remaining & consequently here I find myself collaborating with that awakened sleeper of a poet, putting lines to an inky Cobain triptych to decorate a corner of the cathedral of Book ov Ain't, astonished of its architecture, serving as the foundation for my own humble application of image to some of its surfaces, suddenly observing myself in the blitz of one of the poem's barroom mirrors in the guise of some graffiti writer at the complex of temples to be found at Philae in Nubia (back when the Byzantine Empire was still in her training bra).

If the ancient Egyptians viewed death as travel to regions Westerly (to die as a verb, as in to die is: to go Westing), Crossley's art exists somehow above, which is to say: North of West. It's not Ain't exactly; it is of a Book. Of a book, from the book:

"The history of man is a short / And violent affair / Plagued with wars and hopes unrequited / It's not enough to mark on the cave walls / To just scrawl silhouettes / In some crude cuneiform / As a hasty recording / Of a condition." The poet's Ain't represents much more than "not enough." Like any poet worth more than a grain from the pillar of salt that Lot's wife left through looking behind, that is to say: by not only becoming but composing himself, Crossley has written his / the / our future from the all of our ashes, collective dooms be damned.

JT Dockery

North of Me

By August she'd grown north of me
back to her usual concerns
                  and Lake City.

A summer fling
        is a fickle thing
                after all.

With just a scant few weeks to catch one,
A summer affair sounds mythological,
And as feeting as a firefly

      If fireflies lit wood pallet pyres
    And set city blocks on fire
             Then it's magick.
          Just like that.

(I can remember July. still. The heat. Palpable. Her sun kissed legs propped
up on my dashboard. In my old rotten truck, and her riding shotgun; with my shotgun.)

A summer bookended by smoke.

By June we were on the streets, confused why no one would listen.
They reacted in kind by hurling smoke
And it stuck low between the high~rise buildings
Choked us out from the safe spaces we had created to care for our friends
We were corralled

To wherever they wanted us to end up.

The bicycle brigade held strong.
Creating lines we previously did not have
And block by block we realized the tactical futility
Of being between buildings
With all of their gas.
            With all of their smoke.

By August she'd grown north
          this was still barely June.
We met in file
    Backpacks full of goodwill, granola, water,
It wasn't warm yet. Hoodies and shemaghs
We marched slowly up Pine as the bicycles did their work.
That first night, we made the precinct.
 Sneaking celebratory tall boys in an alley,

 we cheered

We are driving our own narrative
        Beautiful stranger, I think we got this.

(Come July, it would be hot, it would feel like summer. I'd be picking her
And her friends up to learn how to shoot. She'd be wearing cut~off jeans and be bare-
foot .A country song on the radio. windows down on a long mountain road.)

It was barely just June

When we finally took the park, then the precinct.
Still chilly and clad in hoodies
We flushed the tear gas out of each others eyes that first night
after we fled to the SU campus away from the smoke

We made plans
We would not be this unprepared again.
Gas masks and guns and hot meals. HAM radio crash courses. Medical supplies.
Undercover escort for targeted folk
Whatever we can do to keep the fight going

It was June, it was cold. we marched behind Teslas. We rallied behind local rappers.
We made out in shadows through our black masks
Anonymous.
Back in June, I didn't think it'd ever get hot
Not like that
    That wasn't what we were there for.
    That wasn't what we had come out to do.

(When July came in, it came in a scorcher
  It was unraveling from the top down
We spent entire days in a country song on mountain roads
White Claw had a supply shortage, so it was Rainier and Merle.
It was bubbles and Waylon
It was Sprezza and Lorde
We'd lie beside the fire ring and fuck like we were saving
The entire human race.)

So when August came in with its requisite smoke
        And she had grown north

The dit's and the dah's of our personal revolution
Went right up with it
To join that other smoke now strolling in from the Olympics

By August she'd grown north of me
 Back to work
        And her usual concerns
              Up in Lake City

It was hot but it was filtered through a lens of haze
        and no one swept the debris where we had once smashed barricades

(CHOP/CHAZ/BLM protests, Seattle 2020)

Dog Salmon Aristocrats

The first time they built Seattle
                They built it out of wood

And it burned.

Seattle of the saw mill
  Seattle of the deep cold sound
They cracked the tops off of mountains
Like wiping the foam from a mug of keg beer
And they fell the totem like Fir.
They shored up the tide flats and the lakefronts
They shaved the trees from off their foothills
Left swaths of fire break in their wake

Searching for some northwest passage

They trampled through the brush
To build clapboard brothels along the log roads
to brew strong ale inside of lean~to's
They gill~netted salmon by the ton
Stuffed it thick with grease into tin cans
they
      Paddled canoes to New York Someday.

On Earth As It Is.

The second time they built Seattle
                    They built it out of war

And it bombed.

The battleship Nebraska, dry docked and scraped
Of barnacle
Lying in the stink of fish rot. Casualty of the tides.
There were once the old gods here,
            Forced up from granite and tectonic plates scrambled
It appears that iron now holds absolute dominion.
      Some destiny manifested. Yet, the passage
                  Don't exist.

          There is a light on the end of the pier
            Casting a wan candle out to
              That cold and bottomless
                  Sound.

Still, Seattle's name sings loudly
      Shouting off time from the chorus.
Still, Sealths sups come freely
      Still, Seattle's drinks pour cheaply
Where dog salmon aristocrats once shook their cocktails
    With glacier chunks and pine sap.
Where salmon skinned dandies once dined on dog steak
      Their skin crackling off the lamplight
           like fish scale catching rays through
river rock.

The third time they built Seattle
              They built it out of amplifiers

And it rang.

They stamped albums like tin cans full of fish
'The sound from the Sound', this final frontier.
           It don't get more north
              Or west
             Than this
Long haired Lothario's clad in buckskin
        Heaving that sexy axe.
And swinging it round
          And swinging it round
            As to fall the mighty fir, and the granite that lie beside it.

The Skid Road began on south First Street

           And then it dragged into the Sag.

Plank wood stages propped on saw horses
        Still short one Sakajawea
         Searching for a
       northwest passage
That might not actually exist.
   Seattle changed the spelling of his name
          So as not to give him power.

 singing cowboys still bereft of taking one single sober gaze across his ranges

On Earth As It Is.

(chop down the tall trees
plane down the mountains
shore up the lakes
until everything that was magical
is now wholly mundane

the Cascade and the Olympic
       the Duwamp, the blackfish
to the Salish. totems to largesse under the
       rain shadow

The fourth time they built Seattle
          They used tech for brick

And it glitched

…

Hungry Heart Montana

Through these
Triggering towns
I carry a terrible reputation

I can't always fly
   Not to the x's that they mark for
me
That's part of the problem.
     Not always
Bu it's usual enough to be casual

I fall

     For the girls that could destroy me
      For the girls who stamp out the cherries
       Of their cigarettes
        With particular aplomb

 A quick glance across the map
   There ain't a thirst trap I don't go trampling off into.

    Before these girls
It was needle drugs and powders
It was jails and courtrooms and church basement rooms with
Folding chairs where last names were not spoken
  In those basement rooms
They liked to throw out that old caveat

'Don't replace one with another'

And that's part of the problem with folksy philosophy
they're always saying something
And they're not half as wise if they don't see how there's a difference

One will take your teeth

    And the other will take your life

Dangerous girls that can totally destroy me
    That's my
    drug of choice

And there are exactly three beautiful
Girls in the entire city of Billings Montana
One that could destroy me
And another I could take or leave but
        Only one that won't give me the
          Time of day

And there are only thirty nine beautiful
Girls in the whole state of Montana
Twenty that might compel me and three that could destroy me but
        Only one that wouldn't give me
          The time of day

I carry a terrible reputation to the
    City of Missoula Montana

Not a single dangerous
Beautiful girl
Will flirt with me

I've got snakeskin boots on
A truck full of books and possibilities
Parked out there in the lot
We could do anything/be anyone

I've got cowboy boots on and
Great credit as verified
By seven plastic cards
That allow me to chase my
Favorite fix

There are exactly seven beautiful girls
In the city of Bozeman Montana
And if I still had any other

Drug of choice

In a city like Bozeman
I'd be shit
Out of luck

I carry my terrible reputation into every town in the entire state of Montana
And when your drug of choice is
Beautiful girls that could
Completely end you
Every town is a triggering town

I take my shit kicking boots and terrible reputation west to
   Anaconda Montana
  Not a single beautiful snake to be seen

I take my craving north to the town of
   Hungry Horse Montana
I take my truck and my guns and my books
 All of my jewelry laced like totems
     To catch eyes under the beerlight

North/northwest
Into the town of Hungry Horse Montana
With a hungry heart and my immaculate credit score

Into the town of Hungry Horse Montana dropping bullets off of the loops on my gun
belt
Dropping guns on the barroom floor at last call
There are absolutely zero beautiful girls in the town of Hungry Horse Montana
Past midnight in this tonk where the honkies bleat and yawl

   And it's last call
   So I already know
    the time of day

Dog Salmon Aristocrats 2: Nintendo in the Land of Black Tar Heroin

The people once were fishermen and lumber splitters
now
they pull their Toyota trucks off of
Old Highway 99 to ogle
A drive~thru barista in her bra and panty set
Pulling espresso in a utility shed.

moss

moss eats everything in the northwest

(Tahoma
mother of water)

Eventually

rot
eats the youth in the corners
of the bikini baristas eyes

(Tahoma
T'uxt'xw
mother of water)
rot eventually envelops you whole in the pacific northwest

Moss. eventual as in actual.
Rot. Rust.

Mold.
Mycelium.

Out here

where conifers utterly overwhelm broader~leafed brethren
dog lichen and cascara
dross. loam, and basalt.
Sitka shooting roots down into the shallow
soil, loose under the rocks.

Band guys in a bar
that passes for
royalty around these parts

rotting alki
rot
   by the by.

Where Gary Ridgeway once planted bone orchards
Along the I~5 corridor,
From Bitter Lake to Angle Lake
Their hollow bones beneath the soil.
Festering gardens of rot, mold
In bloom.

So many dead girls in this northwestern soil
Yet the remains
Of Sakajewea remain
uninterred

These tall trees
And not one low enough branch to hang oneself on
usnea slung from western Hemlock
the moss it blankets everything
what a great old wooden city
To not float against the rising tides.

What a verdant Gommorah
Chief Sealth got robbed of
 just to build
a wooden Seattle

-O
the poor ladies put on airs
nose up and cinched tight in whalebone corset
soccer moms pre soccer and Subaru
they may not be bar girls
any longer, but they ain't giving no mind
to you.
 "it's the moment you stop feeling like
quarry," she says
"that it can get real boring"
Mercers boats long forgotten
or
utterly
unknown.

Local watering hole celebrity
that passes for royalty around these parts
boys from cherished local
 bands that now tend
bars.

The first time they built Seattle
they built it out of wood
and it burned
        and it burned

the second time they built Seattle
they built it out of war
and it bombed
        how it boomed

the third time they built Seattle
they built it out of amplifiers
and it rang
        how it rocked

the fourth time they built Seattle
they used tech for masonry
     dot com reverb rang out over
           the silent sound
             felling trees in both Bainbridge and Bremerton.

they netted cash by the ton
stuffed it into subsidy and investment
sent it off on boats
bound for eastern Christendom
out here where the fir was the first lord
and them old gods, the mountains
held
     absolute dominion.

The heroin, the suicide,
the men who would strangle women
by the dozens
they were all a~coming
but nascent Seattle

didn't know that yet

C'mon cutie, get in,
     this ain't no death cab
        Gary Ridgeway pulls his pick up truck
           into the lot of a trail head and kills the   lights

Rot.
 Moss.
   It carpets until the concrete.

(Mother of water, where is that water?
   Tahoma blanch these
       bush fires)

will this rot blanket me
       eventually?

Jesus Christ Made Seattle Under Pressure

but Jesus was just a carpenter
BPD if not worse
He sleeps among these hills still
ranting on 3rd and Pine.

so if he built it
it was cobbled of pegs and lumber
a rickety contraption
someone stuck a totem pole in front of
and called it a day

so it burned

Seattle of the Subaru, the suburb,
of the soccer mom. Seattle of the Discover Pass
and tech campus. Nintendo
in the land of black tar heroin
and fentanyl.
Seattle of the tent sodden sidewalks
Of the green woods
and cities of lakes
. cardboard condos
sprawling for blocks in any direction.

Super Mario zooted out of his gourd
 on his kart
pulls a u turn on Old Highway 99
to roll up on princess Zelda
in her bra and panties
pulling espresso shots in a depressing
tool shed

on earth as it is in Tacoma

on earth as it is in Spokane

on earth as it is in Gary Ridgeways
pick up truck.

The Satanik Girls of Instagram

What wanton will
What a wisp o' the wind
What a will of the wild

What a Dennis Wheatley
What a Wizard Whateley

With what wit
What a wonder of whimsy
What a cabal
          All sprawled agog

They like to light a red candle in the northern corner
They leave out offerings
Bowls of fruit and ejaculate
     The beacons of earthly bounty

They like a tinge of pain when the swells build
Hex fetishists
To assemble a witch out of twine and sticks
Mispronunciations
Of occult incantations

Angles lit perfect
From the vantage of her selfie stick
She summons the guardian of the eastern watchtower

*

An ancient rite
Usually reserved for spring

But we recreate it in my bedroom
As the leaves fade
      browning on their branches
Abraxas couldn't spell his name
Abraxas couldn't spell his name
      Abracadabra
      Abracadabra
I create while I speak
Thus sprach
This thin being who makes my urge ache

Wispy
Plague waif
Wispy little plague waif
)Pazuzu wasn't real
        That was only in a movie
          Are you sure you understand
what you're doing?(
Occult
Simply means
Hidden
And you've just shown me
      Everything

The apples withering on her altar
The oranges moldering from within
A bowl of tepid fluid
Grown back to dead again
She summons elementals
And
Mistakes them for boyfriends
*
The satanik girls of instagram

Slide into my
DM's
With cute witchy emojis
They fool with dark forces they don't seem to really understand
Thelemic sigils
On the backs of their hands

The letters of the ouija
Tattooed across her belly
All eyes
An oracle
Yet neglecting to sign off in the circle

A Beast!
      Behemoth
Named HET
       Or also just
Amy
       What wraith blew you through
The transom to my doorway
Only to darken it with your
Purple aura
You
Supine in splendor
Awaiting the only gift
My dark art can render
*
A hedonistic hashtag
Wearing the duality of man for hands

The satanik girls of instagram
Abracadabra
Abracadabra

I create while I speak
What I speak creates
Properties transmutate

Shadow becomes form
Darkness begets light

The faint sight of her familiar
Flickers in her phones pixelated reproduction
Her naked flesh open
An offering
The tattoos somehow more
Defined in this lower light

A wax trail immaculate
Like one single red tear of paraffin
Runs over the moldy orange
And into the bowl of tepid ejaculate

Which wraith plague waif
What wrought witch rot
Is this what all your posed rituals have bought
To be an elementals THOT

Two wispy plague waifs
Lay them down in red sheets
Bend them at the elbow
                    Bend them at the knee
Invert the angle just right
                    Until they form
A pentagram

The satanik girls of instagram

Vegan Leather

Seventeen
And I took to the streets

I took to the streets looking for poems
And I found them there
Hiding between bricks
                    Dark blocks in New Orleans

Seventeen
  And I took to the streets

I took to the streets
Searching for drugs
            Drugs and poems
And I found them there in San Francisco

A bacchanal buffet
When compared to
                Ohio's highs

So...

  Back and forth it began
With the seasons
Hitchhiking
Bumming rides
Hopping freight trains

Late summers in Cincinnati
Autumns in NYC

New Orleans until after Carnival
Then sweeping west through Texas then Phoenix
To San Francisco
O~

San Francisco for everything,

    San Francisco for everything else.

We migrated in loose packs
In this strange sloppy slow circle
Stopping long enough sometimes to fly a sign
Find a girl
Get drunk and re~up our supplies
Maybe pick up a few kitchen shifts

Seventeen
And I took to the streets

And the streets in turn
Took to me
SURVIVAL
A badge of pride
Sewn on with dental floss to the patchwork and pins and pyramid spikes
To my filthy
Black denim vest
-full metal jackets shining in the streetlight
  Like some forgotten constellation
    Bullet belts and big black biker boots

Vegan Leather

Seventeen

And I took to the streets and the
National forests
Looking for words, poems, skills
Hoping to glean some meager means of survival
And the setting to begin my story
And believe me
My story found me

Seventeen
And I made friends on the streets
We formed loose gangs
Posses
Cults
Sects
Young drunk pacts we swore to
We'd change our shirts
But never our black denim vests
Never our tight black denim pants
Until the filth
The grime
The dirt
The blood
Cum
Vomit and
Greasy hands
Put a sheen upon them

Oily denim so grimy that it shone
Under streetlight
That's what we called

Vegan leather

Seventeen and
"Punk As Fuck" we all denoted what we ordained
To be cool
Already spiked up and pissed off at this world which offered us nothing
Armed and amped up on amphetamine,

Flip knives and chains
Padlocks knotted onto bandanas
Stolen pistols and sawn off baseball bats
Heavily armed
Street dregs
Readymade
Patchwork
Militia

We built bombs we got so high
That we forgot about
Anarchist cookbooks
But we improvised the recipes to taste

Seventeen
And I took to the streets

Running
I hit the streets running
Like it was some fresh start

Home ain't
 no disco

It's a transom
Hopped through while forewarned
Sixth and Howard

We left plenty of warnings
Spray painted heiroglyphs
Warded on the walls as
evidence that we got around
Proof
That we we'd left our old hometowns

We wore it on the outside
For the whole damned world to feel

Seventeen
When I learned how to run
Seventeen
When I pledged my allegiance
Seventeen
was a bit young still
                to deal with the

Piles.

A seventeen year old body stuffed in her sleeping bag
In a pile
Left like trash
In the corner of a second story room inside
Some squalid squat in San Francisco
Somebody went ot a hardware store
Pilfered a bag of fertilizerer
To cover her

A pile

She was a simple OD
Traveling alone

No one knew her or knew who to call
I'm not certain that her family ever found her
Or ever understood it was
Only just that

A simple OD
Only a pile

Seventeen
On the streets
Still
        just children really

Vegan leather

Our only armor
Our only tool

I suppose theres times
Where the only thing you can do
is

Bear witness.

How to Cook a Chihuahua

Sad Boi Pozole:
1 part man or small dog, spatchcocked and rendered
4 G. yellow beer, Pacifico works well
3 limes, quartered and zested
1 coconut, milked
4 hot chiles, seeded and diced
1 C. sea salt
2 t. tear salt
bring to boil under direct sunlight and set to simmer for a few days.

*

I was in Mexico

old Mexico, like woven blanket and dog breath Mexico
old Mexico, like dirt roads, deep ditches, and dust in your mouth

I was in Mexico
in a dog town
dog~eared and worn down
around the edges
I came down here so I could drink my head around you
so I could either forget
               or acknowledge you

'It does not cost much. It is pleasant; one of those almost hypnotic businesses, like a
dance from some ancient ceremony. It leaves you filled with peace.
But it takes a lot of time. If you can find that, the rest is easy'

an ocean of yellow beer

for me to surf you out on
and old Mexico never
disappoints in terms of beer
or sun
to bake my head
melt my glacial winter ruts

Of course I blame myself

  Running thousands of miles away as I do
To sit on this beach and stare at these stars the ancients once used to chart
Entire spanses of oceans

  I don't recognize a single constellation

And I can't even sit here and decipher from their
Patterns if I should stick around
      Or if you even love me.

Of course I blame myself

      Even this Crab Nebula
Is not as nebulous as I am
  and every single star that supernovas
      I blame myself for.

          So

  often in winter
      I wander to old Mexico

south
    souther

southest

and for getting these dogs to
bark on cue
accept no counterfeit
or substitute.

I went down to dog tongue Mexico
so I could learn how
to stop breathing through my mouth
maybe write a poem or two
the idea being
that when you're underwater
it's more of a lung technique

I'm supposed
to hold my head under
and not breathe

only
supposed to hold my head under the water
    only
       supposed
          to
           not
             draw breath or fight it
                   for a few brief moments

       no mames guey

it's just a yellow ocean of beer

Lo siento pierritos

36

my tongue still lolls the same
I pick the grit of sand from between my teeth
and wag there
licking wounds
like the stupid dog
that I am.

(Quotations from MFK Fischer, How to Cook A Wolf)

Invocation of my Demon Brother
(for Jason Morris)

 He had read the Book of Thoth
and
 the Book of the Law.
He had created Scarlet Women out of high
         school girls
Always some tome or sacred edict
to grant him further direction

Menstrual Blood Cum Cakes

The first thing he ever cooked that wasn't a cheese sandwich

 Afraid to taste it first he fed them to his rat
and his pet rat went crazy
hiding underneath its bedding for the rest of its days

If every man and every woman is then indeed a star

         rats

are only that when spelled in inversion

The Star in that West set a bit askew

Jason refused
         to use a toothbrush
and instead opted to wipe his teeth with his t shirt

38

Wild eyed
and mercurial when drinking
he was almost brilliant
Of course
we both knew
we were bound
for one magnificent adventure

40 days through the desert.
like Crowley and Neuburg
He was going to love this new freedom I'd just found
The drugs, the dubious legality,

The altered reality.

We bought new books and edicts;

Fighting in the Streets

Urban Guerilla Combat Tactics

Improvised Explosives and Other Dirty Tricks

ordered from the back pages of
    Soldier of Fortune magazine.

We practiced
some odd formula of black ritual magick and urban survival
Bucklands Compleat Guide to Wicca
led to the streets and practical tactics
Moonchild
The Book of Lies
Behold a Pale Horse

anything by
Bill Cooper
or
Jeff Cooper
        and the Paladin Press catalog
a cassette tape dub of Penis Envy side A
and Operation Ivy side B.

Then

We learned how to squat the forests

        us;
    true survival boys/lost boys/wild boys

learning how to pack calories from leaf teas
and armed with weapons from a gun show
we'd spend weeks in the Daniel Boone Forest
Practicing
Rehearsing for our Huck Finn on hard drugs revolt
wandering towards West Virginia

just knives, cord, e tools, and a tarp.
just 2 handles of Early Times whiskey
just hunting squirrel with a crossbow

no jobs
no money
no sense

just book smart

but lucky

40

so damned
          lucky that
we had girls to look out for us

cum
menstrual blood
olive oil
dandelion flour
and allspice

Jason's Crowley Cum Cake recipe(gf)

the only thing besides
Top Ramen
he knew how to cook

All of the possums in West Virginia
couldn't save him
nor could all of the salt in the sea

he slouched off towards Maine
to pluck bugs from the ocean floor

all of the possums in West Virginia
sing a wistful Sunday choir
and sprout little wings to carry his soul
off into the fields of Elysian
and over the vast waters
of Lobstricity

all of the opossums in Appalachia
now adorned with tiny tin haloes
and white robes

pockets slung low with Stephen King novels
and a sudden urge
for song
strum toy harps with marsupial paws

so mote it be

hax pax max deus adimax
hoc est enim corpus meum
transubstantiation
and other bullshit
ochus bochus
an aeon of horus
the whole of the law
do whatever feels

his teeth now as sharp and as brown
as his crazy pet rats
as holy as them appalachian opossums
his aether sputtering off to oblivion
in a little wisp of opium smoke

An
Invocation of you
my demon brother

The
Cobain
Tryptich

Washingtongue

I chose among the Cascade mountains.
 The hill I want to die on

Their jagged peaks
Offer a certain peace
I'd never found previously

To the west
          The Olympics puff their chests
Their foreboding snow capped doom
          My Jericho
My fortress
               My chosen
And closing in like a great stone embrace
          When I get the itch to roam

So much water,
               And so close to home

Low hum depression
Everyone I know lives with
Guess it's just northwest

Down in Seattle
Around the docks the fog
Can sit still between the buildings in the mornings

The silent sound in shroud

A great green lawn of water
It's fathoms a host
  To eldritch beings
Sentients of the city
        Who watch over our town with
Cyclopean vision
        Their gangly tentacles
    Snaking through
                The avenues
        And up
                The hills
    Like tendrils
                Reaching out for
        Searching for
                A keep

Arcane tech
        Our town
Prehistoric electric
As if the occult and the profane
Were scrawled both on the same page
An urban sprawl alive with nature
                Creeping ivy grabbing skyscrapers
                By the ankles and searching
                Like those cyclopean tentacles
                For the throat

To be at once a lumberjack
A hacker
A witch hippy
 And a billionaire

And to know
 It was almost Andrew
But it took him too
        The depression and desperation
That gets swept off of the mountain peaks
To join the snow melt in the spring
And forever cascading
        Down
Into our tap water
Until we willingly drink this thing which kills us
Use it to sow our crops
Use it to water our poppies

Gray
Gray looms large on the palette
Of the pacific northwestern painter
Gray is our camouflage
It's in our flannel
In our bones
In our songs

Gray is the color
Of rainwater on campfires
The meter of our haiku
Our grim understanding
It's our ink
When we sign our lease

Monstrous
Red octopi
Sea creature deep await
Sasquatchian legends
Of some of the greatest words ever writ

Until the hill
You want to die on has grown mountain

Floodplain fields
    Lay fallow
Ebb tided   X'd out through the leaden days
That blot out most of the calendar
From interstate to salal
Grayshale growing like great thorns
From the verdance

"If you drive an hour in any direction"
They like to say
On days when they like to say anything back at all

Steamboat Slough in February
                    Francis Farmer still interred on Bainbridge
Staring out of her only window
                    Liquor in her milk
                    Liquor in her orange juice
She won't starve this winter
                    God dies, but Frances knows
    This city eats its own

Dreamboat tough
            Ain't it Annie

That cyclopean eye
Myopic

Old Man Winter
he's
A motherfucker

Kurt Cobain
Put the shotgun barrel to his mouth
Ripped it like some dorm room bong
One April morning
That year that the winter lasted too long
Sitting there high
     So high
In the guesthouse of his
Madison Park mansion
Looking out over his rented expanse of
Ashen
Smokey
Lake
Like Francis Farmer looking out of hers over the sound

The mist
So gray
Like camouflage

Ain't it Annie
    Ain't that where we hide also

I can only wonder if he was lucid enough
             To have a second thought
                Exactly one moment after
              Setting that 20 gauge
            In its place

          Kicking off his famous sneakers
       And curling his big toe through the trigger guard

Maybe it's just the Seattle thing
That famous freeze
Verisimilitudes bricked up behind
Insecurity and flaw

That northwestern nod
                    No reciprocation at all

Walking from bar to taproom
Looking for a friendly face
   A place to root
To choreograph conversation
Not slumped over the stool staring
At your phone
Surrounded by people yet unwaveringly alone

 No man
          Wishes to be the type of man
                    That the city no longer needs
A poem is an anachronism
          In this age of memes
And when the whole of human language
Gets reduced
To 140 characters or less
One can only make
              Haiku
Of the rest

          What is it with the winter here
 How it curls like smoke around your hollow bones
Envelops you wholly

Until there is only
The weak January sun to guide you
Through the gloam

So much water,
and so close to home

Any stance you take
And charge banners to the summit
Defend it
Because it's your home
That's the hill you chose to die on

****
On EArth As It Is IN TaHomA

****

jtdockery 2016

The La De Dadaist

"What is life you ask
What is death I ask
I give them both my buttocks
My two wheels rolling off towards Nirvana".
                    Anne Sexton

Hey Skeezix, something has been on my chest
Hey Skeezix
Does the audience want their poets
Depressed

And gloomy
        No room
For the softer hues of contentment
Do the readers like their writers
At the precipice of suicide
or over

Imagine reading a happy Sexton
Without the yawp and the yaw

The bloody mundane drudgery
Of house wifery

Lowell's class in
            a different Life Study

'Astral planes and pockmarks do
Wax a certain pull'
Waning stars
Under microscopes
Do they want us warts and all

What is a song
But a desperate confession
A hoarse and throaty
   pleading
          at the stars
And what is the writer
But another lost actor
A voyeur
       A cheap peep show John

Skeezix
I know I know
La de da

April 5th 1994

I was in San Francisco
             With my girl
We had a habit and a problem
She hadn't had her
       period
in two months and it wasn't the
Drugs

As we were hoping after all.

Sitting outside of San Francisco General

Smoking cigarette butts off of the sidewalk
And waiting for her to walk out

I had heard the news in the waiting room

Kurt Cobain found dead

And my girlfriend came out of the sliding doors crying

I didn't know she was even a fan

But no
It was the photocopy

The sonogram

The nurse saw fit to give to
Homeless street users

As if it might change our minds

vacuum our bad life choices away

Toss us down some correct path to parenthood

Almost a father on the day that Cobain died
I found myself equally as depressed

A mercury retrograded in
Perpetuity

Throw la de da's at Skeezix
    Throw Dalai Lama's at nirvana

Like bowling blown~off heads down hallways
There will always
Be room to grow

O
Skeezix
Of all people
I wouldn't imagine you
To be upset

The voices of entire generations
Muted by their own hand

And then come carrion
To pick clean the remains
Snatching fecund seconds
From them holy roller bones

O
Skeezix
Of all people
I'd imagine that you
Would understand

****

catching zzzz's

****

Four Wheels Rolling Off Towards Nirvana

zzzzzzz
    zzzzzzzz
       zzzzzzzzzz

sawing logs down in Aberdeen
the most depressing scene
    I've ever seen
what a hoary pastiche
      this leaden season

(In the dream
we're in a black convertible
Burning through the desert
a few hours east of Seattle
Cobain is riding shotgun
And he doesn't have a head)
That wasn't supposed to be a joke
Funny

Funny

He was just riding shotgun
With no head

What kind of junky
Kills themselves when they still
Have dope left?
Or the money to get more?

Apple,

An apple

Like numbers and incantations an apple
Has several meanings

A company that turned wood into tech
An album that Wood killed himself a month
Before releasing

A tempting snack offered by a bundle of hiss
In the garden

An Apple

A garden variety noun
Several paths
Chosen
To make this logging town into something

It's either a trite coincidence
Or
        it's

absolutely everything

And the Cascades become the actual
Tower of Babel
Before crumbling to shale and rubble
At the cornerstone of commerce.

Ok

Okay
Ultra
Mega

(when the dream began
        I'm leaving Seattle
in a black convertible
destination Spokane
it's just past dark on the lost highway
I see the figure of a man on the roadside
sans head.
his thumb out sheepishly.
He doesn't need to have a head for me
to recognize him
even without his face intact
there's an aura of those blue eyes.
I pull over to pick him
up)

Kurt Cobain 2023
 short hair
Shorn amateurishly
Washed out in pink and green
Splotches
"Corporate rap sux"
Tattooed in fine line
Along his right eyebrow
His addiction
 not a dirty flaw
Secreted away behind vague verses
His drugs of choice
 tattooed in baby blue
 across

His throat

He made his name
His initial streams came
From a love letter to opiates

"Suboxone Orange/Summer Sun"

Xanax
Does his PR

mosquito libido indeed.

Is that bright of a star
So intoxicating
That you have to die for the high?

I'd rather crash
Like Darby
If I were trying to die
All artsy

When punk rock
Grew bored of being scurrilous
It expanded it's repertoire
Picked up different hobbies
But it couldn't just shove a safety pin
Through the internet

(in my dream The headless singer
slides into my passenger seat.
Even in the dream I can recognize that
this figure shouldn't be headless.

He used birdshot in a 20 gauge
which even at that close of a range
would render everything inside of his skull
to applesauce, but the skull would remain
in fact.)
in tact.
Mad Season
           was playing on the radio
I didn't plan it like that
it was just a dream
it was just the way the mix played out

zzzzzzzz
    zzzzzzzz
        zzzzzzzzz

Sawing logs down in
Aberdeen
The most depressing scene
I have ever seen

So let me burn in some Boise foyer
Let me wander some Spokane winter
Let me pick the light
In the dark that connects the stars
               After all
                  Every man
                     Inherits a desert of his own device
        Every man gets to choose the hill
              Upon which he wants to die

All of us like to fuck
Like we think we invented it

A real
Soft shoe dance
Around the blue romance
Of a true jazz drug

Like
Heroin
Like
Heroin
Like
Heroin

-Say it
Place the word into your mouth
And allow it to bloom on your palate
Allow it to loll
Back near the root of your tongue

On your
Tongue
On your
Tongue
On your
Tongue

Even the vowels
Copulate there

The word itself
is like fucking something forbidden

The yonic on the phallic
Yet it is

    not sexual
  That word.

So just close your eyes and let it roll

let it roll like those four wheels on
    on HWY2,
        straight on through
    passing.   Medical Lake

Heroin.

yeah.
    I get it.

(in the dream again, I inform my silent
passenger that I'm headed to Spokane.

Remind him that he's free to ride with me for that long.

That I am in love with Washington
but Seattle has just gotten so…

  but Seattle has just gotten so…

and without words or gestures

  I can tell that my passenger

      gets
         it
           too)

40 Days to San Francisco (a squatter punk lent)

Two anarchists by the onramp
Kingman Arizona, April 21 1995.
We had been loitering there for twenty days
Ron Jones and I.
Flying a cardboard sign that read
"San Francisco"

then finally

"Anywhere"

It had taken us twenty days to make it this far west from New Orleans
where we scattered after Carnival
across Texas
            then north to Arizona.
Almost a month of no beer
        sans smack
We had no way of knowing we'd be observing some kind of DIY Lent.
Going on forty days with no money
no tobacco
no forties.
and coming out of New Orleans
where even the fantastical is tangible
we could turn heel and walk right back
order us an oceans' swell of yellow beer.
All of these days sober
        dry
the desert is dry

the desert is sobering.

Nothing but parched bones in the valley
sun starched litter tousled up from the dust
by the constant passing cars

two anarcho punk junky Odysseus's
trying not to stick out like sore thumbs
Dean Moriarty and Sal Paradise in greasy black denim with our thumbs stuck out
on that Kingman Arizona highway entrance.

Three days after Kingman Arizona's most
famous resident parked a rented Ryder truck stuffed with
 5000 pounds of ANFO explosive
 outside of the Alfred P Murrah Federal Building in neighboring Oklahoma,
killing so many.

The cars passing
lolling us into an artificial rhythm
 whipping past
the traffic now all black Crown Vic's.
blacked out windows,
blacked out wheels.
some with their sirens on
others silent, prowling Rt. 66 like packs
of canines
In an ocean of cops
inside of a sea of dirt and sand.

Two squatter punk Odysseus's
with the good sense to avoid Feds
 standing out on a desert highway now paved with police.

Anarcho punk Sal Paradise and Dean Moriarty on an accidental lent

40 days and 40 nights in the dirt
DIY
a gutter punks lament.

wanting nothing more in this world than the street kid paradise that is the sidewalks of
San Francisco.
A cold forty ounce of beer
and a nice warm spoonful of smack

The Great Southern Northwestern

Decatur to Toulouse where the
poems write themselves

some batshit ratchet
gator bait girls
piling out of a bootleg cab
on the corner of Royal
makeup smeared from tears
        now forgotten
by a deluge of shots
plastic beads lace their necks
in garish resplendence
dollar bills pinned to the red heads
lapel tells me
it's her birthday

Magazine to Rampart
where the poems write themselves

Graham is a bartender
So he hates Modern Love
he tells me that when you're a bartender
you have to hear it all the time
in his estimation
it's a tired story he's heard
too often.
Hippy Johnny to Ol' Skydog
Damn man
we get this far south I want swamp rock
and sawdust on the floor

guitars strung from gut
　　wound through alligator jaws
or just this here
　streetcar

Burgundy to Muses
where the poems write themselves

A dancer, pole and all
on the roof of a van.
　　From our vantage
the strippers pole reaches
as high as the steeples
those stiletto heels kicking high
to poke holes into heaven
and letting a little bit of a lovely night
drip through the cloud cover

Frenchmen to Decatur
where the dogs walk themselves

I'd grown so tired of walking the floor
pining over you
so I nailed my left foot to the floorboards
walked in small circles the rest of
the night.
Flew into the arms of
the fleur di lis, that local crucifix.
We found some friends
down there among the
ancient brick and iron work
so improbable it's wrought

    one scant whisper of home
and I found myself feeling
not so weird or alone
anymore

Felicity to Carondelet
where the dogs walk themselves

Florida girls with occult tattoos
cast binding spells into my DM's
their instagram incants an anchor
but I flow constant and steady
like that wide Mississippi river
no spell to bind me
no thirst trap to vex me
like an errant beer bottle cast into the river
I'm just floating by
I'm just passing through
And if the mighty Mississippi turns
ouroboros
I'll always be floating back to you

Saint Charles to Euterpe
where the bar never closes

We flew in with
typical northwestern glower
ordered one of every drink that has ever been made
the bartender informed us that
he don't deal in absolutes
to which we both replied
how delightful

it
  is
      down

    here

*

Salt and Pepper Punk (reasons I take Berman in Moderation)
***

She lives on can beers and bar fruit
fingernails for texture
and a cigarette to
punctuate.

I think we've both seen an
      intake

Me
I shiver away my mornings
on my nice couch
for falling asleep in my jeans
and boots on

again.

old punks in the bar light
Toulouse-Lautrec
Crescent City turnaround
and a bj to boot

southern hospitality

feels like love
curt; yet courteous come morning.

Just two weeks ago we were in
        New Orleans
      and now we're back here

on the west coast again

        old punks
who never stopped wandering.

If I could runaway with you
I would've left already
            but
    there's nagging needs
                echoing in this soon
            back from where I stay.

Finding love in your 40's
is like finding love in your 20's
except it's a lot harder to
scramble eggs the next
 morning
            lest that mean something
                lest she mistakes breakfast for an invite
                    to stick around a while.

I'm sorry but
    you got to go in the morning.

I made a mountain out of
a fleeting feeling
        now the view is so nice
it's difficult not to stare at it
        to take it all in

        mountain ranges are gorgeous
                to gaze upon
            a treat to think hard about

                    but
        it's not a human matter what
             created them/what tumult
              bore them to be
        (My view from this breakfast nook)

Finding love in your 40's
is a lot like finding love in your 20's
except now you have good credit and cash
and can afford to travel by plane
you have toilet paper and clean towels
and never even run out of beer money
you do your laundry
the enemy in your interior is dust
or
lazy jags

If you're going to bang around these scenes
as long as me
        you learn to DIY your self esteem

You chose to live alone with your records
and posters from old shows you
played or attended

the only thing to draw breath in your house
            was a choice
not a plant nor even a cat
the only thing living in your nice apartment
are the fruit flies
and sure,
        they buzz around your head
like a halo some nights

and sure,
>   sometimes that feels holy

old punks in the barlight
weary of love
Salt
and pepper punx in their twilight
>   to lose all track

She lives off of beer tabs and bar fruit
tequila sunrise and an uber ride
to Tukwila
and we probably got more in common
than we don't.
So I'm going to play a few more
Silver Jews songs on this jukebox
and watch to see if she sings along

us old punks man
we might not die
but we sure as fuck don't
moisturize

To always
 Speak in these
monosyllables
like some code that ain't cool
Just so tired
>   of being misunderstood

Finding love
  is like finding love
>   in your forties

Closing Night at the Clown Bar

Closing night at the clown bar
And it was filled
With girls I dated
When I first moved to this town

Closing night at the pinball bar
And my first love
In this entire city was there
She smiled when I walked in
no sign of alarm bells behind her eyes

There she was
Only barely graying around the temples
A true queen of Belltown
A pinball legend

She asked me about my poetry
And I confirmed
That
Yes
I'm still chasing poems
that sometimes masquerade as women

Closing night at the clown bar
I went and it was filled
With awkward
Exes

all of them

I felt
Guilty

exposed

Closing night at the clown bar
And I ran into old lovers
the room a swirl of circus and black metal
and we laughed about the things
that no longer matter
We had the barstool conversations
That I had been missing for so long

Things I would've said were I less toxic
then

Closing night at the pinball bar
And I am
So happy
We got caught up

Hey, I miss you

You've still got it
You're a force of nature to behold
you play pinball like no other

And you
And you as well.

Hey

Take me out of this place
it's great to catch up but its
Making me feel rather anxious
let's just you and I
find a quiet corner
in another neighborhood

Feed me amaros and stroke my bruised ego

Lets toast to our futures
And i"ll pick up the tab
To apologize for my pasts

Closing night at this pinball bar
I'm pink to find
that
We're all still friends

Single Occupancy

So this is it?
        This is the distance?
This self absorbed seething.
           Sitting numbly dumb staring at moving pictures on a screen.
As foreign as this all seems.

               Hearing words echo between your ears
               Still beating. Dumb as doldrums.
         We attempted to build a home
         From smouldering sticks and a moon on the wane
            Now only the ink remains.

It's often hard to think it all through
           Compartmentalize
Single
In a town full of
 Single Occupancy Studio Apartments
It can get difficult sometimes
             To find the space to spread out
When you know what distance meant
In a studio apartment.
When there is archaeological evidence

Of structures built that were greater than this.

In a single occupancy studio apartment

When you knew exactly what
Apart meant
The space that you needed divides entire city blocks

Far too long to comfortably walk
And the space you needed won't leave
                              A trace
When the space you needed
                    Turns into space.

And space is a black and cold and ever expanding
      And space is a cold and long
            And space is always further never nearer
                  As space pulls you away from the sun.

So this is distance?
Two celestial bodies floating through aeons
Two points in mid air
                  Never touching
                        Never crossing paths
                              Never near enough to even notice
Thrown up in the ceiling fan and left to scatter like crash.

Is the space that you wanted really all of this space that you meant?

SINGLE OCCUPANCY STUDIO APARTMENT

They always say that you can't come back
            But you can
            Yes you can
You can always come back to this
            They'll say you can't
            But you can

Yes you can
There will always be a small room for rent

space ship man

When the space that you needed
Is as vast as the cosmos
And as open and empty as the air near the ceiling of this apartment

But with what violent urgency?
With what suffering subtlety?
Which one will wash out?
Which one will stain?
There is archeological evidence of great civilizations

Where now only the ink remains.

And this is the space that I wanted
And this is the space that I need
An apartment who's hallways are haunted
Who's occupants shamble and bleed

They say you can't go back
But you can
They say you can't go back
But you can
Yes you can
Space man
There will always be a room for rent
SINGLE OCCUPANCY STUDIO APARTMENT

Anxiety in the Age of Memes

Sorry Ian Curtis
But if love tears me apart
Even one more time
I'll be naught but a shredded sheet
Stuck on a fence pole
Flapping in the wind

Blacker than a bible
The winter night fell
Passing empty taverns
Closed saloons of empty stools
On a slow solitary walk home

Used to be a writer
Now mostly just a drinker
But boy
Had you seen me back then
You'd swear
I could've been a contender

Just shove what you're feeling down
Cover the blemish with a
Metaphor so you won't ever have to face it
As it is

The history of man is a short
And violent affair
Plagued with wars and hopes unrequited
It's not enough to mark on the cave walls
To just scrawl silhouettes

In some crude cuneiform
As a hasty recording
Of a condition

Hasten the morning
From a night as black as catholic fashion
On a movie set of Moscow
Where you broke in to drink amaro
In the turret bulb of a fake kremlin
But it was just drywall and wire
And couldn't take your weight

I am sorry Ian Curtis
But if love tears me apart
Even one more time
I will cut out it's tongue and plant
Death seeds at its root
I'll kick a pike between its ribs
And puncture it's ruddy lungs
Leave it facedown in the mud
As a corpse of outmoded necessity

The history of human love
Is a short and violent affair
We beat on cave walls with bones
Until we hitched a rhythm we could ride
Through a black as flint ash night
Until the morning breaks with the suns true warmth
Used to be a writer
Used to be a lover of some renown
Now I acquiesce
To the back of the cave with the drinkers
The barkers the blinkers

Wide eyed and wasted
The true bastards whose fathers stay unknown

Go ahead Ian Curtis
Let your love tear you to shreds
Normally I'd say you can find me at the bar
Spinning myself in small circles on a stool
And my dizzy walk is still a strut
If you look at it in the right light
I step away from a red square soundstage
Where the wires were never hung right enough to glide ballerinas in wings
If the love of anything
Ever tears me apart again
I swear to Christ
I'll kill us all

Mikey the Kid

I used to be that kid
Sitting on the sidewalk with a pen
So inspired by what transpires
Scratching out frantic poetry
As the city
Blossomed around me

I used to be the kid
On the side of the highway with a thumb
Catching trade winds as they blew
In any which direction but home
One desperate month in Arizona
I held a sign that simply said
ANYWHERE

I used to be the kid
On the off ramp with a sign and a dog
Bandanas around both of our necks
     "Spare change
     Anything helps
     God bless"
We had found through extensive research that
Adding the
   God Bless
Resulted in fifty percent
Greater returns

I used to be the kid
With a pilfered Kinko's card account

84

Cutting and pasting
My sketches and prose into
Provocative broadsides
Half of a swastika shoved down

The throat of Jesus Christ
  Who was actually Charles Manson
    The swastika comprised of veiny hard dick
  pasting my cut up prose with occult symbols
    fashioned in Sharpie hand style
And stapling this
To every telephone pole in town

I used to be the kid
Scouring the alt-weeklies
In every new city
Looking for the open mic nights
I'd tie my bandana
Tupac Shakur style around my head
And wait my turn
Get on the stage and read my hot five
Then beg the audience to buy me
Beers
I considered this my job

Like a Cartoon Wolf

Like that cartoon wolf
tongue rolling out of my mouth
like a red carpet
like rolling out the red carpet

heart beating visibly three feet out from my chest
Like that cartoon wolf
mouthbreath
mouthbreath

awww oh gah
awww eewwww gaahhhh!

I was born like this
born this way
and it looks like all of these years in
it ain't gonna change

I have an eye for the ladies
the gemini and the Aries
Like that cartoon wolf
my canine desire
like begging for table scraps
woof
woof
woof
Like that cartoon wolf

Bodies in its wake
Bodies in its wake

Is there a lupine lust
that does not leave bodies
on its path

Everything you believe in
Faith
entire systems of worship
can be eradicated by a girls kiss

It's a Tex Avery animation

that ain't blood

it's a cartoon.

ahhhh oh gah
ahhhh ewwww gahhhhh

steam blowing out of each of its ears
as that long red tongue lolls
salivates there

just

dripping.

What rough beast
slouching towards the singles bar
slinking down the summer sidewalks
propelled on its own steam

hackles raised

I'm just as dangerous
as a cartoon wolf
just so you know before you neuter and declaw me
my bite not so rabid
photo realistic
              mostly demure
not this panting
               pacing
cartoon
      cur
looking for some way to salivate
without leaving
bodies

bodies

      in my wake

First Hill Sleeps Alone Tonight

Too much zenith in my azimuth, too much yaw in my pitch

These girls walk up and dump trauma
leave it sitting in my lap
like a pile of something
stinking

Meanwhile

my friends,
medicated genius' and celebrated satanists,
pharmaceutical amigos they take sexy selfies on a gurney.
they tease their hospital gown up high
            to show off thigh, cheeky in their triage
mi amigos
    graying with jokes.
      (no fans, got to pay their own bills for the advils)

we used to call it baggage;
            what they label trauma

they dump it and then undress on the internet
become bashful after the act
Nam vet stepdads gift coins
as I run my fingers up the dress
of the suicidally depressed

and all of the trauma girls
            transfer their bar tabs

All of my brilliant friends, long distance drinkers and drug addicts all. ex members of
dead bands and defunct cartoon strips.
pharmaceutical amigos dying alone and left like Lefty.
          Cold in Ohio

(I'm from the Nam vet generation, the pre natal PTSD pre cum of that whole mess
We learned not to rely on much help coming even from our own,
how to make do in the field
how to walk quietly through your parents
home knowing that any sudden noise could
make your father snap in a burst
of sudden
sharp
 violence)

pungi sticks in the mosh pit,
Lake City quiet pills dissolved
     in tin cans of Rainier beer

They want me to make them cum
          I just want to make them better

               but lo-

          I ain't drugs

then these trauma riddled girls go ahegao
and I forget the age gap

Too much zenith in my azimuth,
too much yaw in my pitch

90

Hot girls with mental health issues
my own personal Vietnam

My friends, pharmaceutical amigos with rooms full of old merch from dead bands.
CD's and tapes, t-shirts and stickers so old they lost their tacky entirely.
The trauma girls snap a pic of their toes, bottle their gargled milk and I reinvest
yes, we:
Pharmaceutical amigo and me.

The trauma girls can't even
 doom scrolled
 doom posted
 doom seeded

My brilliant friends didn't dim as they grayed, diminishing their bulbs in myriad ways.
His room in the hospital looked just like the green room backstage. Lefty left there,
just a note on the page. My old amigo in his Suboxone days.

Long distance drinkers, my friends,defrocked dick priests, and talented junkies

And all the trauma girls don't go fund us

Too much zenith in my azimuth
                    too much yaw in my pitch

Mosca Avacada

I never met you
Mosca
You were my best friend Ron
Ron Jones
We of the shitty kitty cat neck tats

The rockabilly street punx
who never had a dollar
but always had grease and a comb
(and a Jawbreaker mix)

you hid it
like you thought I'd care
after all of our miles together
you should've known
I don't live that way

*

God dammit.

*

we were supposed to grow old
together

you were supposed to start
that wiener dog farm

in North Kentucky
all 1000
of them named
"Buttons"

so we'd pop a beer at feed time
and you'd just holler

"Buttons!"

and the pitter patter scatter
of one thousand
dachshunds
would swell the earth with dust

*

I knew quite early in our travels
that you weren't into
girls
you could've had plenty
of my run off
and I sipped freely from
all of yours

I didn't care then
and I never did
I tried to offer you some alternative
to such polarities

Homey
I see you in these social media memorial posts
that I shirk from

these days
when I miss your voice/your being
I youtube you

*

I love you

*

We were supposed to get
a plot of land in
bluegrass county
KY
make our own beer
farm dogs(your dream not mine)
live on our own steam
load our own ammo
and just write
poems

Sometimes I feel
I'm the only one left tending this farm
still holding the same dream dear
still writing shit poems

I don't know why you thought
that I would care
or treat you any differently
I am not now
and I ain't never been

*

94

I'd have loved to have met you
Mosca Avacada.   by the way;
I think you're name is
downright brilliant
It's certainly less North Kentucky
than Ron Jones Junior

I was glad to hear it
when you settled in
NOLA
I can watch you
in a loop
when I search it on youtube
happily pedaling
your bike down Royal

*

You were in Asheville
North Carolina
last time we had contact

I was in South
Carolina
typing out one more chapbook
before I died
before I took that final shot
last call

I was certain

withdrawing among the spanish moss

made it seem like a
faraway issue for
a month

I was supposed to/
and you were too.

but neither of us did.

You said the notoriety
from the documentary was too much

That people treated you as
"King Hobo Punk"

and that it felt
off set

But you still had Chessie
your only anchor to familiarity

*

I didn't make your funeral
but I heard a train stopped
the entire procession
      (I was sick… crawling my floor back
         in Ohio
       openly weeping that I couldn't
       summon a mere $20 to pull
         myself back together)

*

We were supposed to get old and angry
together
    Mosca
We were supposed to talk shit about
      the young punx
   on the porch we both shared
hating all of the new music
and still
     even at this advanced age
       combing our hair back with

Murray's Superior Pomade

and arguing about Jawbreaker
   and whose poem about fog
 coming in on Embarcadero is most accurate
*

I'll never cover the shitty
black cat tattoo on my neck
Even though it's faded Mosca
even though I started covering
all of the rest of them
It reminds me of us

*

And I ain't never want to let you go

Smudge Sticks

Even wars have terms

So my dear
Then must this
Because I see you in your corner
Pumping yourself up like a pugilist
Banging your fists together
Baring your teeth
Pacing
        squaring up

Like you're about to knock everything out
Everyone who knows you
knows
You ain't got the energy

Your kind of war
I'm well defended for

I've honed a well practiced apathy
Into the shape and fashion
Of a blade
(like some convict that has to share a cell with you
Trying to protect myself,
A shank)

I see you there

Over by your banners
Donning armor
Preparing for a siege
Some engine of destruction
You've bolstered yourself up against

Hey there
       Joan of Arc

There's no enemy on your soil
To you
 Belong these spoils
Some royal krieg
        To some grand decree

And you charge on
          And on
             And on
                And on

And on again

Until your foes all fell
    run through by pikes

You're foes were faceless and legion
And you
Could not sleep
      Could never rest
Until they were all slain by your blades

But

They may as well be ghosts

Because they are dead

Or they do not exist

Gamahauche

Thick with shit
  a Victorian kiss
hot breath lathered with drool

Thick with hiss
  a Victorian kiss
suckled from teat of empire

Unbrushed and brown
        gin
      stained
      and
      tainted

Bound tight by bodice and stinking of
     rat fur   and sweat

While Queen Bodaceia
        ripped to ribbons on the flagstone

and bled out into the brown water of the Thames

and bled out into the head water of yellowed crown

gilded
Gelded

What a golden age!

In the age of reason and diety
that those two might coexist
      the river rank with piss

Thick,
  that shit
     on a Victorian kiss
gamahauche of sweat and squalor

Yeats himself could not enlighten

  Blake's own dark castings*

END

BOOK OF AINT

Last Chance Saloon(a reprise)

when you're young
  you believe
that
    time
will heal all wounds

because you're young
    and time
      is the only commodity
you possess in any sort of surplus

This is not a room created for being seen

    or attracting a partner in

this wooden bar is not a scene

it's a dour room
    created for drinking

solemn drinking

    not different than a church
      in form and utility

to outside passengers there's only two
    neons shouting out to the
         downtrodden

the one in red reads
    "cocktails"
  and the other
    "open"

much like a wilderness tabernacle
      might have a barren cross
  to boast its wares

there is a row of stools for parishioners
 to alight themselves upon

or mimic heavenly choirs

glossolalia occurs on these stools
      if not as often, then as close to
        as it does on local pews.

***

Highly
Decorated
Veterans
of
Honky Tonk
Wars

***

When you're young
   and all you have is time
      you of course

         downplay

      this time.
    (being young and all)
    it's the only thing
    you currently have
      any amount of

so you waste a great deal of it
   trying to look cool on barstools
   and not get caught looking at

yourself

      in the back bar mirror.

Besides,
   you came into this adult world
    armed with the only knowledge
     you can wield as a weapon

(Time heals all wounds)

106

except
   that's bad intel
      in that time doesn't heal shit
         not like what you're thinking it will
            it won't

There are churches

  cathedrals built to dwelling on it
thou mayest discover

   (timshel)

a
  barstool
        serves a
            certain
              duality

in these raw wood
        saloons
it's not unlike
      frontier churches
roughly hewn wood worn smooth by butts

stale peanut eucharist
genuflect in reverse

and hold the puke inside of your mouth
until you reach the urinal
teary eyed and red

Last call absolution
another forty dollars
an indulgence.

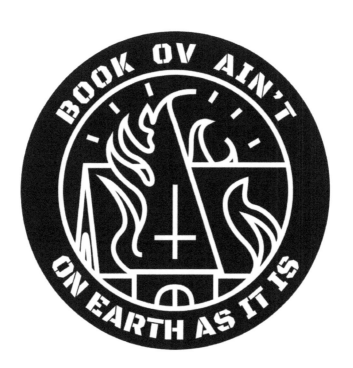

Michael Crossley is an executive chef, writer, musician, and spoken word performer currently residing in Seattle WA. This is his fifth published collection of poetry. His previous titles include Still Life… With Drinks, and Some Girls received positive reviews in the regional literary scenes of his home (Ohio, Kentucky). His last chapbook, Dead Letters 843, was turned into the debut album In Tongues by the band French Letters. Much of his early work is archived in the Weston Gallery in Cincinnati and some of his marker tags can still be seen in certain pockets of the cities mentioned herein.

Milton Keynes UK
Ingram Content Group UK Ltd.
UKHW050018080823
426465UK00004B/8